GLOBAL GROOVES

EXPLORING WORLD RHYTHMS, SONGS AND STYLES

BY WILL SCHMID

TABLE OF CONTENTS

HAL•LEONARD®
CORPORATION

7777 W. BLUEMOUND RD. P.O. BOX 13819 MILWAUKEE, WI 53213

Copyright © 2014 by HAL LEONARD CORPORATION
International Copyright Secured   All Rights Reserved

Visit Hal Leonard Online at
www.halleonard.com

In Australia Contact:
Hal Leonard Australia Pty. Ltd.
4 Lentara Court
Cheltenham, Victoria, 3192 Australia
Email: ausadmin@halleonard.com.au

IN HAVANA

LESSON PLAN BY WILL SCHMID

LEARNING THE RUMBA

On the Island of Cuba (in the Caribbean just south of Florida), the *Rumba* (ROOM-buh); sometimes spelled "rhumba") is a popular style of Afro-Cuban dance that has roots in both West African music and the music of Spain. There are three basic types of Cuban rumba: *Yambú* (yahm-BOO), which you will be learning, *Guaguancó* (hwah-hwan-COH), and *Columbia* (coh-LOOM-bee-yuh).

LEARNING SEQUENCE

1. Teach the Rumba Drum Ensemble "Easy Parts." Optional "Challenge Parts" may be added given time and sophistication of the players.

2. Learn the song, "In Havana," (p. 4) in both English and Spanish. Add the second harmony voice part when students are ready.

3. Perform the piece together with the full performance recording (CD track 1), the accompaniment recording (CD track 13) or perform live with percussion and voices.

4. Study Cultural Connections as you progress and as time permits.

LEARNING THE RUMBA WORLD MUSIC DRUM ENSEMBLE: EASY PARTS

The Rumba Drum Ensemble has three "Easy Parts" and three "Challenge Parts" that can be added if time permits and players are ready. Avoid trying to teach both the Easy and Challenge Parts at the same time. Teach the parts to everyone in the following order. Those without an instrument should play on their thighs or desks.

1. The **Shekere** (SHAKE-eh-ray; large gourd rattle with beads/seeds and netting on the outside) can be played by any rattle, but a small or large gourd with external rattles will sound best. Play on the beat by hitting the gourd against a hand or thigh. Use this part to keep everyone together.

2. The **Low Conga** (say the word, COOK; then put that double OO sound into COONG-guh) may be played on any medium or low Tubano or conga-like drum. The first three hits with X-note heads are played in the center of the drumhead with a softer, muffled sound — just let the hands fall onto the head. The last hit, played at regular volume, is a high tone played on the edge of the drumhead. Use the indicated hand pattern of

L-R-L-R or its reverse R-L-R-L. Have all students think or say these syllables as they play: Boo-bah-doo-BAH. This will help them learn faster. When everyone can play this Low Conga part, add the Shekere on the beat and play along with the recording of the song.

3. The **Easy Sticks** are played on the sides of the drum shell or any other wooden surface. Have students practice this part by using their forefingers of each hand as sticks and playing on a desk, book, or the sides of a drum. The stick pattern (can be reversed) is crucial and must be carefully monitored. Start by having everyone play on the beat (with the Shekere) with their left hand — this never changes; then add the right hand hits to the on-going left. As you play, have students think or say these syllables: *Doo-bop-bah-doo, Doo bah doo.* You only need a few stick players. Start by selecting those students who can handle this part with ease. Then put all three Easy Parts together with the recording of the song.

SINGING

1. First teach everyone how to sing the melody together in English.

2. Then teach the whole class the Spanish translation as follows:

    En La Ha-ba-na, (ehn-Lah-BAH-nuh) ["La" and "Ha" are elided to sound "Lah"]

    to-can la rum-ba (toh-cahn lah ROOM-buh)

    con la con-ga (cohn lah COONG-guh) [the "oo" in coong-ga is pronounced like "cook"]

    y el ca-jón. (ee-ehl-cah-HOHN) [see Cultural Connections on next page for *cajón*]

    Se sien-te el rit-mo (seh see-EHN-teh ehl REET-moh) [practice this triplet rhythm often]

    de la rum-ba, (deh lah ROOM-buh)

    se sien-te la bri-sa (seh see-EHN-teh lah BREE-sah)

    en la can-ción. (ehn lah cahn-see-OHN) [the two syllables of "ción" are quickly elided]

3. If time permits and students are ready, teach the Voice 2 harmony part. Point out the common use of parallel 3rds or 6ths (the inversion of a 3rd) in Latin American music.

4. Sing these parts along with the recording.

Drum Ensemble

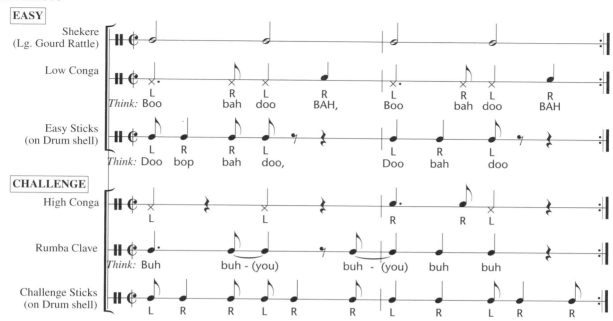

Learning the Rumba World Music Drum Ensemble: Challenge Parts

You may add some or all of these Challenge Parts according to the sophistication of your students. If players are struggling with the Easy Parts, it will not help to add more parts. Add them in this order.

1. The **High Conga** may be played on a high Tubano or conga-like drum. The left-hand hits with the diamond-note heads are played in the center of the drumhead with a soft, muffled sound — just let the hand fall onto the head. The right-hand high tones are played on the edge of the drumhead and should sound louder. Once you have both the Low and High Conga parts playing, you should hear a melody between the two on their high tones.

2. The **Claves** play a so-called "rumba clave" part which is the timeline for the whole piece. It sounds a lot like the typical 3:2 Latin American clave part, but the third hit is a half-beat late. Here is an easy way to teach it:

Rumba Clave

Think: Buh   buh-(you)   buh - (you) buh   buh

Then in the same rhythm say only the "buh" syllables, whispering the "you."

If you then clap your hands or play the claves on the "buh" syllables, you will be accurately playing rumba clave. If this part is added, put it in the hands of your strongest players.

3. The **Challenge Sticks** part just adds more to the Easy Sticks part. Notice the left-hand and right-hand sticking. One player on this part is usually enough.

Cross-Cultural Connections

In Cuba, dockworkers started playing on wooden crates and later created the *cajón*. Some even rattle like a snare drum.

Find someone in your community who knows how to do a few easy rumba dance steps, and teach them to your students.

Find these recordings and play the Rumba Ensemble along with them. (Some are rumbas, and some are not): "La Rumba d'el Jefe," "Café Mocha" or "Havana" by Jesse Cook.

Cuban *cajóns*

3 Projectable & Printable PDFs on CD
Drum Ensemble • Guitar/Bass • Piano

GLOBAL GROOVES

IN HAVANA

Words and Music by
WILL SCHMID

Rumba (in 2) (♩ = 92)

mf 1st time, sing top notes only
f 2nd time, add bottom harmony notes

In Ha - va - na,— they play the rum - ba——

— with the con - ga— and the ca - jon. Feel the

rhy - thm———— of the rum - ba,— feel the breez - es——

— in the song.———— En La Ha - ba - na,— to - can la

rum - ba———— con la con - ga— y el ca - jón.

Se sien - te el rit - mo———— de la rum - ba,— se sien - te la

bri - sa—— en la can - ción.————

WEWE NI MUNGU WETU

LESSON PLAN BY WILL SCHMID AND DAVID LEE REYNOLDS JR.

"Wewe Ni Mungu Wetu (Unaweza)" is a song from Tanzania, a country on the East Coast of Africa. This song began its life in the church but quickly made its way into schools and the general public due to the song's highly addictive melody and powerful meaning. It comes to us by way of David Lee Reynolds Jr., music teacher in Vienna, VA. The first verse to the song, Unaweza, translates as "You are able, Lord."

LEARNING SEQUENCE

1. Locate Tanzania on a map of Africa and learn about its history and traditions.

2. Teach the easy *Unaweza* chorus of the song; then teach the other sections.

3. Teach the Drum and Rattle parts to the World Music Drum Ensemble.

4. Teach the optional Recorder parts.

5. Combine all these parts with the recording.

ABOUT TANZANIA

Go to the Internet and do a Google search for "Tanzania," "Swahili" (official language w/English) "Mount Kilimanjaro" (Africa's highest mountain), "Lake Victoria" (Africa's largest lake), and "Serengeti National Park" (world-famous game preserve). Learn how Tanzania became a new country in 1964 by combining the names of its two parts, Tanganyika and Zanzibar. Challenge students to name the eight countries that border Tanzania (counter-clockwise from north: Kenya, Uganda, Rwanda, Burundi, Democratic Republic of Congo, Zambia, Malawi, Mozambique).

ABOUT DAVID LEE REYNOLDS JR.

Music teacher and co-author of this article, **David Lee Reynolds Jr.** (see photos below) teaches general music to students in pre-school through sixth grade in Vienna, VA. He also is the executive director of **The Vienna Jammers** (www.viennajammers.org), a non-profit percussion ensemble. David was invited to travel to East Africa and serve as musical director for Robbie Schaefer's non-profit organization, **One Voice** (www.onevoicecommunity.org). He has worked with children in Tanzania, Uganda, and Kenya and helped raise funds for various projects to include building a secondary school and helping pay for medical treatments for Kenyan children born with heart disease.

SINGING

1. Teach everyone how to sing the melody of the *Unaweza* chorus at the beginning. The only tricky part is the hemiola (3:2) m. 6, but students will catch on to it easily if you practice it enough to feel comfortable singing it to them. You might find that it helps them to pat the 3-beat on their thighs, switching to a 2-beat for m. 6; then back to 3 in m. 7. Repeat till everyone can sing the melody with ease. The Swahili words are:

    Unaweza (3) bwana (Oo-nah-way-zah bwah-nah) = You are able, Lord.

2. When everyone knows the melody to *Unaweza*, you can introduce the harmony part (bottom notes) that comes in next. This part is a very logical second part and consists mostly of parallel 6ths below the melody. If your students are ready, the other harmony part (middle notes) may be added. Both of these harmony parts are optional. If male voices are used, have them sing either the

melody (top notes) an octave lower or bottom notes in the same range as the altos.

3. The *Wewe ni mungu wetu* verse section is led by the Lead Voice (or small section). At the end of each phrase, the Lead Voice gives direction for what is to come next. This technique is related to **call and response** and an old song-leading style referred to as **lining out.** When the Lead sings *Imba wewe* (Sing *wewe*), so all sing along on the following *Wewe* section. When the Lead sings *Unaweza* instructing everyone else to sing the *Unaweza* section. When the Lead sings *Imba unatosha,* an instruction for all to sing *Unatosha bwana* to the original melody. Notice throughout the piece how the Lead Voice tells everyone where to go next. Since Tanzanian singers mostly sing orally without written music, lining out is an effective technique. The Lead Voice also sings some countermelodies above the rest of the chorus throughout.

The rest of the Swahili words, pronunciations, and meanings are:

Wewe ni mungu wetu (Way-way nee moong-oo way-too) = You are our God.

Imba wewe (Eem-bah way-way) = Sing "wewe:"

Imba unatosha (Eem-bah oo-nah-toh-shah) = Sing "unatosha:"

Unatosha bwana (Oo-nah-toh-shah bwah-nah) = You are enough Lord.

Sema (Say-mah) = Say: *Wewe ni kibilio* (Way-way nee kee-bee-lee-oh) = You are our refuge.

4. When singers are ready, try singing along with the recording (CD track 2).

LEARNING THE DRUM ENSEMBLE

This World Music Drum Ensemble has only two parts, and both of them can be played while singing.

1. The **Medium Drum** may be played on a Tubano or other conga-type drum. Play all notes below the line as "low" tones in the center of the drumhead. "High" tones, notes above the line, are played on the edge of the drumhead. Note the right-hand and left-hand indications. The R and L hands may be reversed by any player. It is important to teach drummers to do a specific pattern and not just "their own thing." Start by teaching players to play the R hand only on beats 1, 2, and 3 by saying "low high high." Then add the L hand. Sing the first half of the *Unaweza* section while playing. When the 3/4 pattern is solid, move to the 6/8 feel of m. 6. When players are ready, practice alternating between these measures. Then sing the *Unaweza* melody and put the drum patterns in their proper place. Note: the hemiola measure is not played during the *Wewe ni mungu wetu* sections.

2. The **Rattle** part may be played with any rattle, but it will sound best if played on a shekere-type gourd rattle with netting on the outside. Practice the rattle with the singing, changing the pattern in hemiola measure. Note: the hemiola measure is not played during the Wewe ni mungu wetu sections.

LEARNING THE OPTIONAL RECORDER PARTS

The first and second Soprano Recorder parts use easy-to-play notes. Be careful with the F# fingering (T 1 2 3 _ 2 3). The Alto Recorder part is also optional, but it will add to the overall sound.

Drum Ensemble

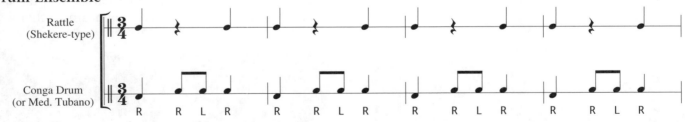

(Hands: R = right, L = left; hands may be switched.)

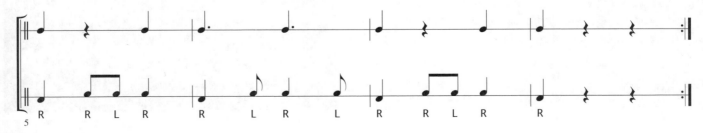

OPTIONAL GUITAR AND BASS PARTS

The Guitar part is written to be played finger-style (p=thumb, i=index, m=middle, a=ring finger), but less experienced players may just strum the chords. The Guitar/Bass part may be played on any kind of acoustic or electric bass.

CROSS-CULTURAL CONNECTIONS

There are many recordings of music from Tanzania available on iTunes. Following are some of the album titles worth checking out (*=favorite):

- Chibite, *In Bagamoyo–Tanzania Africa*
- Hekima and the Bongo Flava, *Sonrise*
- *Hukwe Zawose & Master Musicians of Tanzania, *Mateso*
- Motuba, *Bongo & Harp (Jazz Elements)*
- Singer-Songwriters from Tanzania, *Kibagamoyo Wabagamoyo*
- Tanzania House of Talent, *Three Years On…*
- Wagogo People Tanzania, *Sing to the Well*

5 Projectable & Printable PDFs on CD
Guitar/Bass • Drum Ensemble
Piano • Recorders • Full Vocals

2 & 14

WEWE NI MUNGU WETU
(UNAWEZA)

Rhythmically (♩ = 120)

Traditional Tanzanian
Arranged by WILL SCHMID
and DAVID LEE REYNOLDS JR.

1st time: Sing top notes only
2nd time: Sing top and bottom notes only
All others: Sing all three notes

U - na - we - za, u - na - we - za, u - na - we - za bwa - na, u - na - we - za, u - na - we - za bwa - na. U - na - na.

Verse — *Solo or small group*
We - we ni mun-gu we - tu, Ni mun-gu u - na - ye - we - za. Im - ba we - we

mf All
We - we ni mun-gu we - tu, Ni mun-gu u - na - ye - we - za. U - na - we - za.

FORM:

Chorus: Unaweza *(three times, each time adding a voice)*
Verse *(Solo, All)*
Chorus: Unaweza
Chorus: Unatosha
INTERLUDE

Verse *(Solo, All twice with soloist improvising)*
Chorus: Unaweza *(twice)*
Chorus: Unatosha *(twice)*
Chorus: Unaweza
Chorus: Kibilio *(twice)*

DOMIDOW
A PAPUAN SONG FROM INDONESIA
LESSON PLAN BY WILL SCHMID AND ANITA ARDEN

Two separate countries govern the island of Papua. The east side is an independent nation called Papua New Guinea, or PNG for short. The west side is a province of Indonesia, and is currently called West Papua. From 1963 until 2002, it was known as Irian Jaya or West Irian, and many Indonesians still call it that. The native population prefers the name "Papua." Prior to 1963, it was known as Dutch New Guinea or Netherlands New Guinea. "Domidow" is known and sung by the Ekari people of Paniai in West Irian as well as the Ayamaru people, who live in the southern part of the Bird's Head peninsula. Both tribes have had contact with Christian missionaries for a number of years.

LEARNING SEQUENCE

1. Find the Island of Papua on a map and learn about the people and their culture. Learn about Papuan teacher, Anita Arden, and her students.

2. Learn the melody to the song, "Domidow." Add the second harmony voice part if students are ready.

3. Add the simple movement steps to the song; then put them together.

4. Learn the two drum parts. Put them together with the singing.

5. Add the mallet parts that sound best on metallophones (xylophones may be substituted, or the "for rehearsal" piano part, PDF found on the enhanced audio CD, may be played).

6. Study Cultural Connections as your progress and time permits.

LEARN ABOUT WEST PAPUA

Search online for "West Papua map Indonesia." You should be able to see the map in various forms including a satellite view. Notice how close it is to Australia. The western part of the island looks like a bird's head, and this is the region where the song is sung.

Music teacher and co-author of this article, **Anita Arden,** teaches at an international school and also has responsibilities at a local Indonesian school. Here are a few comments from Ms. Arden about her location:

The community I live in is near the Kamoro tribes. The closest Indonesian town is Timika. They have some fascinating drums — very long, with a handle in the middle, hourglass shaped, small head. The skin varies with the animal available. I've seen them with snake or lizard skin, as well as goatskin. I have a blog at http://anitaarden.com. It has some information about the schools, pictures, and also an example of Kamoro dancers and drums. There are about 250 separate languages (not dialects) in West Papua. During World War II, General MacArthur based himself in West Papua (then known as Dutch New Guinea) prior to his invasion of the Philippines.

SINGING "DOMIDOW"

The translation of the text for "Domidow" is from Matthew 7:7–8 and is "Ask and it will be given to you; seek and you will find; knock and the door will be opened to you" [8] "For everyone who asks receives; the one who seeks finds; and to the one who knocks, the door will be opened."

Pronunciation of the words is similar to many European languages where "a" = ah, "e" = ay, "i" = ee, "o" = oh, and "u" = oo. The word "tai" is pronounced like the English word "tie," and "kai" rhymes with it.

Sing each phrase and have students echo. Give each note a slight separation:

5̄5̄ 1 · | 1 5̄5̄ | 3 · 3 | 2̄2̄ | 1 2 3 | 3 | 3̄3̄ 3̄3̄ | 3 · 3

Do-mi-dow *[Doh – mee – doh]*

A-ni da-mo to-pa tu-ghu-tu-ghu tai
   [Ah-nee dah-moh toh-pah too-goo-too-goo tie]

Ki-da-mo *[Kee-dah-moh]*

ke-ba-i *[kay-bah-ee]*

ke-ba-ya wi *[kay-bah-yah wee]*

A-ni ki yo-ko ya kai
   [Ah-nee kee yoh-koh yah kie]

Indonesian choirs often learn to sing parts by reading numbers rather than notes. The number 1 is treated as moveable "Do." The first two phrases of "Domidow" would look like the above.

When students have learned the melody, you may wish to add the second voice part. Another option would be to teach the movement below. Then teach the second part. Voice parts may also be practiced with the metallophone accompaniment.

MOVEMENT

Moving to "Domidow" is very easy and completely logical. Here are some comments about Papuan movement:

Papuan music always has movement with it, and the movements are generally small and simple. This dance begins on the first note of the song, and it can be done either stationary or traveling. Knees should be slightly bent. On the forward taps, the weight-bearing knee bounces slightly with the movement. Arms should be bent at the elbow, with the elbows held away from the body, and the upper body should twist slightly with each weight change.

Here are the steps. Practice them in place first (R = right, L = left, T = tap).

The movement in line two is exactly like line one.

Do-mi-dow, _____ Do-mi- dow, _____
 R - L   R   T   T L - R   L   T   T

A-ni da-mo to-pa   tu-ghu-tu-ghu tai. [Repeat 2 lines]
R - L R T T T L - R   L   T   T hold

Ki-da-mo ke-ba-i _____ ke-ba-ya wi _____
Stop motion _____

A - ni ki yo-ko ya kai.
R - L R L   R L

Practice singing and moving together, either in place or traveling.

DRUM PARTS

Combine the two drum parts below, teaching each one at a time.

Add the drum parts to the singing.

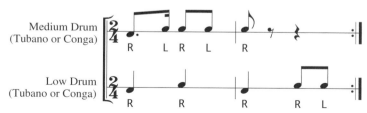

Medium Drum (Tubano or Conga) 2/4 R L R L R

Low Drum (Tubano or Conga) 2/4 R R R R L

Hands: R = right, L = left; hands may be switched

MALLET PARTS

Play the mallet parts (PDF on enhanced CD) on metallophones if possible, but xylophones will also work. Long notes may be rolled at the discretion of the teacher. If mallet instruments are not available, the "rehearsal only" piano may be used.

COMBINING ALL PARTS

Put together all of the parts. If students have trouble holding their pitch during the opening section, you may add either keyboard or you could double the parts with SM and AM2.

CROSS-CULTURAL CONNECTIONS

If time permits, study some of these Indonesia instruments and ensembles; photos, video and audio sources can be easily found on the Internet.

Gamelan [GAHM-eh-lahn] orchestras from the islands of Java and Bali consist of many players playing a variety of mostly percussion instruments including knobbed gongs, metallophones, xylophones, double-headed barrel drums, flute, and/or strings. Gamelan orchestras may accompany puppet theaters known as *Wayang Kulit [WHY-ahng koo-LEET]* or dance. The shimmering sound of the gamelan is like the metallophone ensemble in the arrangement.

Angklung [AHNG-kloong] bamboo shakers are single pitched and work in roughly the same way as a bell ringer ensemble. Players often hold two shakers with a different pitch in each hand. Anklung ensembles also play by the numbers.

3 Projectable & Printable PDFs on CD
Drum Ensemble • Mallets • Piano

DOMIDOW

Traditional Papuan
Arranged by WILL SCHMID
and ANITA ARDEN

Do-mi - dow, do-mi - dow, A - ni

da - mo to - pa tu-ghu-tu-ghu tai. Do-mi - dow,

do-mi - dow, A - ni da - mo to - pa tu-ghu-tu-ghu

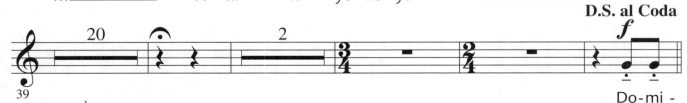

tai. Ki - da - mo ke-ba - i ke-ba-ya

wi A - ni ki yo-ko ya kai.

D.S. al Coda

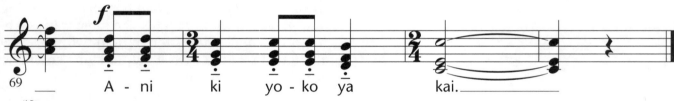

Do-mi -

CODA

mo ke-ba - i ke-ba-ya wi

A - ni ki yo-ko ya kai.

DOMIDOW

Traditional Papuan
Arranged by WILL SCHMID
and ANITA ARDEN

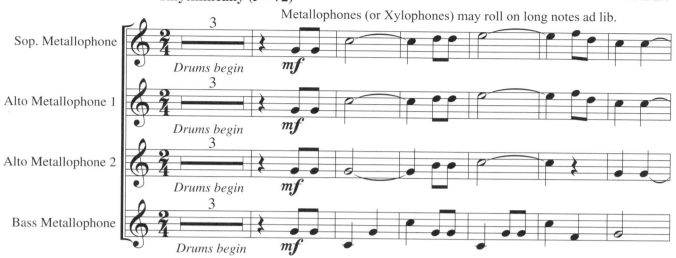

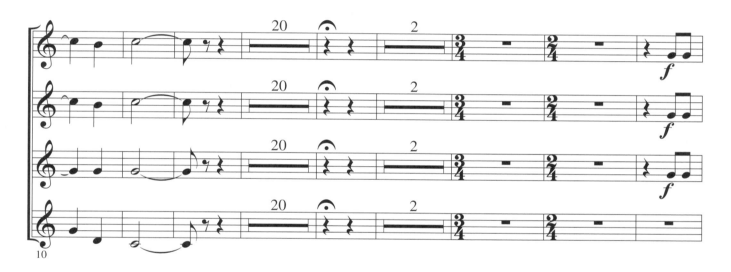

GLOBAL GROOVES

THE CZECH-MEX POLKA

LESSON PLAN BY WILL SCHMID AND KAREN SCHOOLEY

When styles of music transplant themselves to another part of the world, interesting things happen. This was the case with the German/Czech/Polish/Austrian polka when people from this region moved to Mexico and (what later became) Texas. When you listen to some Mexican *banda, norteño, conjunto,* or Texan *tejano,* you would swear you were listening to German polka — except for the Spanish lyrics. "The Czech-Mex Polka" combines two well-known songs, "Muss i' denn" and "El rancho grande," to help explore this cultural connection.

LEARNING SEQUENCE

1. Locate Germany, Poland, The Czech Republic, and Austria on a map of Europe. If time permits, research online maps of this area in about 1830-1870. Then locate a map of Mexico and the Texas border. Also explore maps of this area from the nineteenth century.

2. Teach the basic boom-chick or oom-pah rhythm on a drum with a stick.

3. Teach the song, "Muss i' denn," in German (or sing neutral syllables).

4. Teach the song, "El rancho grande," in Spanish (or sing with syllables).

5. Learn how to sing chord roots (with bass runs) like a tuba.

6. Combine all these parts with the recording.

GERMANY/THE CZECH REPUBLIC/ POLAND/AUSTRIA

Two of the best-known dances to come from this region are the **polka** (2 beats: oom-pah) and **waltz** (3 beats: oom-pah-pah). Study maps of this region and see how the names and boundaries have changed from 1800 to the present.

MEXICO/TEXAS

Study a nineteenth century map of Mexico (that includes Texas). The ***banda*** (pronounced *bahn-dah*) style of music features accordion, brass, woodwinds, and percussion and became popular with German-Mexicans in the northern states of Mexico around 1880-90. Two currently popular bandas are Los Remis and El Coyote y Su Banda Tierra Santa.

Norteño music also features the German-influenced polka style with the main instruments being the accordion and the *bajo sexto* (guitar with 12 strings).

FAMILY TIES

Ask students if any of them have family backgrounds that connect with the German/Czech/Polish/Austrian or Mexican/Texan locations being studied in this lesson.

LEARNING THE DRUM ENSEMBLE

This World Music Drum Ensemble has only two parts, and both of them can be played on one drum while singing. The **basic polka beat** is often called "boom-chick" or "oom-pah." It can be played on any drum (or a desk, box, or water bottle). With the weak hand, play a low tone on every beat ("boom, boom, boom, boom") in the center of the drumhead. With the strong hand holding a stick or pencil, play on the offbeat on the side of the drum shell. This should result in a steady sound like "boom-chick, boom-chick). When students can play this with ease, try it with the recording of "The Czech-Mex Polka." Then split the class in half and have each half play one of the two parts. The tougher part (the off-beats) can be made easier by having students whisper "boom" or pat their thighs on "boom" so they know where to play the "chick." Play this while singing any easy 2/4 or 4/4 song that they know. Speed up the tempo and see if they can hang in there.

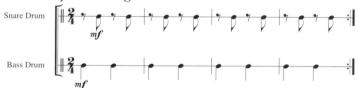

SINGING

First teach everyone how to sing the melody of **"Muss i' denn"** at the beginning of the arrangement. Singing neutral syllables such as "doo" will make it easier to concentrate on learning the melody. This nineteenth century song by Friedrich Silcher is one of the best-known German folk songs of all time. Depending on the time available, either teach the harmony part (Voice 2) or work on the German words. Many of the German words in this song are sung in a dialect which shortens the words: *ich=i'* (English =I), *mein=mei'* (English =my). The words, pronunciations, and translations are:

> *Muss i' denn,* = Moos ee den
> *Zum Städ-te-le hin-aus,* =
> Tzoom Shtay-teh-leh heen-ows,
> *Und du mein Schatz bleibst hier.* =
> Oont doo mine shahtz blybst heer

Wenn i' komm', wenn i' komm', = Ven ee kumm
Wenn i' wie-der, wie-der komm, =
     Ven ee vee-dehr vee-dehr kumm
Kehr i' ei' mei' Schatz bei dir. =
     Care ee eye my shahtz by deer
Kann i' glei' net all-weil bei dir sei', =
     Con ee gleye neht ahl vile by deer zeye
Han' i' doch mei' Freud' an dir. =
     Hahn ee dohk (guttural ch) my froyd ahn deer

English translation: I must leave this town, and you, my love, remain here. When I come back, I will return to you my love. I cannot always be with you though I enjoy it. When I come back, I will return to you my love.

Then, in the same sequence as above, teach the melody, harmony and Spanish words to "El rancho grande." In Spanish, sometimes two syllables are elided and pronounced as one: e.g. *A-llá* and *en* (the *llá* and *en* are pronounced yehn) The words, pronunciations, and translations are:

A-llá en el ran-cho gran-de, =
     Ah yehn ehl rahn-cho grahn-day
A-llá don-de vi-ví-a, = Ah yah dohn-day vee vee-ah
Ha-bía u-na ran-che-ri-ta, =
     Ahb-yoonah rahn-chay-ree-ta
Quea-le-gre me de-cí-a, =
     Kayah-lay-gray may day see ah
Te voy ha-cer tus cal-zon-es, =
     Tay voy ah-sehr toos kahl-zone-ehs
Co-mo los u-sa el ran-che-ro; =
     Koh-moh lohs oo-sile rahn-che-roh
Te los co-mien-zo de la-na, =
     Teh lohs koh-me-ehn-zoh day lah-nah
Te los a-ca-bo de cue-ro. =
     Teh lohs ah-kah-boh day coo-eh-roh

English translation: Over there on the big ranch, where I lived, there was a woman who happily said to me. I'm going to make your clothes like those of a rancher. I'll begin them with wool; I'll finish them with leather.

To teach the above lyrics, consider this strategy: Write the text on a flipchart (or Powerpoint) and teach the text from the chart. Then after they have practiced it a couple of times, start removing words little by little until the whole text is learned. It works so well to learn the text and they are practicing singing the song again and again, but each time with a new challenge. They don't even realize that they have just sung it 10+ times in a row! It's a great motivator for repeated practice.

When students are ready, sing both songs along with the full performance recording (CD track 4) or the accompaniment recording (CD track 16).

Tuba is King (German: *Tuba ist der König*; Spanish: *Tuba es el rey*)

Teach students how the tuba player in both polka and *banda* plays the roots of the chords and improvises bass runs between the roots. "Muss i' denn" uses mainly the I and V chord with a single use of the IV chords. Explain how triads are constructed above a note by skipping every other note of the scale (**1** 2 **3** 4 **5** = 1 3 5 called the **I** chord built on the first note of the scale; **4** 5 **6** 7 **8** = 4 6 8 called the **IV** chord; **5** 6 **7** 1 **2** = 5 7 2 called the **V** chord). Now signal which chord root to sing by using your left hand off to the side with index finger for the **I chord**, your right hand off to the side with five fingers for the **V chord**, and four fingers for the **IV chord** right in front of your body. Have students sing the notes and numbers at the beginning of each measure for "Muss I' denn:"

     I V I I I I V V I I (repeat)

     V V I I IV IV I V I I I I I I V V I I (repeat)

When they can sing the roots of the chords, practice singing these bass runs:
1 7 6 5; 5 6 7 1; 1 2 3 4; 4 3 2 1

Then have them try to sound like a tuba and sing/play along with the tuba part on the recording.

CROSS-CULTURAL CONNECTIONS

There are many good recordings of polka and banda available on iTunes or YouTube. Following are some worth checking out:

- Sepp Vielhuber, *Muss i' denn*
- Whoopee John (from New Ulm, MN), *Muss i' denn*
- Los Remis, *Ando en busca*
- Los Remis, *Cielo*
- Flaco Jimenez & Steve Jordan, *El rancho grande*
- El Coyote y Su Banda Tierra Santa, *Allá en el rancho grande*
- YouTube: Oesch's die Dritten, *Ich schenk' dir einen Jodler 2012*
- YouTube: Mas Energia, *Rancho Grande*

Your students may also want to know what contemporary songs students in Berlin are listening to. Here is a short list provided by Karen Schooley of recordings on iTunes:

- Peter Fox, *Stadtaffen and Haus am See*
- Herbert Grönemeyer, *Mensch*
- Die Ärzte, *Zu spät*
- Wir Sind Helden, *Denkmal*
- Fettes Brot, *Emanuela*

See p. 18 for information about Karen Schooley.

6 Projectable & Printable PDFs on CD
Accordion • Clarinet • Drum Ensemble
Trombone • Trumpets • Tuba

THE CZECH-MEX POLKA

**Arranged by WILL SCHMID
and KAREN SCHOOLEY**

Muss i' denn, muss i' denn Zum Städ-te-le hin-aus, Städ-te-le hin-aus, Und du mein Schatz bleibst hier. Wenn i' komm', wenn i' komm', Wenn i' wie-der, wie-der komm', wie-der, wie-der komm', Kehr i' ei' mei' Schatz bei dir. Kann i' glei' net all-weil bei dir sei', Han' i' doch mei' Freud' an dir. Wenn i' komm', wenn i' komm', Wenn i' wie-der, wie-der komm', wie-der, wie-der komm', Kehr i' ei' mei' Schatz bei dir. Kann i' glei' net all-weil bei dir sei', Han' i' doch mei' Freud' an dir.

GLOBAL GROOVES

EL HUMAHUAQUEÑO

LESSON PLAN BY WILL SCHMID

"El Humahuaqueño" (pronounced *El Oo-mah-wah-KAY-nyo*) is a well-known song from the northwestern part of Argentina and Bolivia that has been recorded by Andean music groups throughout the region. This song is often played on the *quena* (end-blown flute) or panpipes — the featured instruments of the region (Argentina, Bolivia, Peru, and Ecuador).

LEARNING SEQUENCE

1. On a map of South America, find northwestern Argentina where it touches Bolivia and learn about the people and their culture.

2. Learn the melody to the song, "El Humahuaqueño" in the lower octave and add the upper octave for higher voices. Add the second harmony voice part if/when students are ready.

3. Learn the two drum parts and rattle part. Put them together with the singing.

4. Add the recorder parts found on the enclosed enhanced audio CD.

5. Add the guitars and ukulele/charango parts found on the enclosed enhanced audio CD.

6. Study Cultural Connections as you progress and as time permits.

THE SOUND OF THE ANDES

A typical small musical group from the Andes Mountain region may consist of:

Quena (pronounced *KAY-nah*), a small end-blown flute (about the size of a recorder).

Panpipes, a graduated bundle of open pipes played by blowing over the end.

Guitar, or other similar instrument.

Charango, a smaller fretted string instrument with a sound like a mandolin or ukulele. Some charangos have armadillo backs.

Harp, a small portable harp.

Drums of various sizes.

Find and share photos of these instruments with the class. Or better yet, bring in the actual instruments if available. Listen to the full performance recording of "El Humahuaqueño" (CD track 5). If time permits, play one of the recordings of "El Humahuaqueño" listed under Cultural Connections.

SINGING "EL HUMAHUAQUEÑO"

The lyrics to the piece are simply an imitation of the sound of a flute. Notice that the staccato notes are "toot" as opposed to "too" on the half notes at the end of each phrase. The "Lai-la-la lai lai" (pronounced *Lie luh-luh lie*) lyrics also have no meaning.

1. Start by teaching the melody in the lower octave of Voice 1 the A section; then sing the upper octave in the B section. Students should catch on to the melody easily. Then have the higher voices sing the upper octave of Voice 1 in a light head voice that sounds like a flute. Only use the lower octave notes in the B section if necessary. Sing the melody along with the recording.

2. Teach Voice 2 when students are ready. Like many of the songs of Latin America, this harmony part is an interval of a third below (or above in some songs) the melody. Reinforce the concept of the interval of a third by singing up the scale using numbers (e.g. "1 – 2 – 3"); then have students sing "1 – 3" followed by both tones at the same time.

PLAYING RECORDERS

Soprano recorders sound very much like the South American flute called the *quena*. The optional recorder part is found on the enclosed enhanced audio CD. Teach the first half of the Recorder 1 melody by rote (skip the pickup note in m. 4) in the lower octave having students echo each phrase. When they can play this with ease, introduce the concept of a half-hole in the thumb (the thumb opens up half of the hole) that will then produce the upper octave. Repeat the echo process for each phrase. Combine the two octaves. Then teach the second half of the melody in mm. 13-20. Drill on the left-hand finger movements for the notes "B – A – D;" then finish the melody. Combine both halves of the melody and have the upper octave players play the m. 3 pickup note "B." Play with the recording. Add the Recorder 2 part when ready.

Drum and Rattle Parts

Medium Drum (Tubano or Conga)
R R R L R R R L R R R L R R R

Low Drum (w/padded stick)

Rattle (Goat Hooves if available)

1. The Low Drum part plays the same rhythm as the Rattle (hit against thigh or hand). Play the Low Drum with a padded stick on a 14" Tubano, a low-sounding frame drum, or any other low-pitched drum. Any rattle will do, but goat hooves sound especially good. Eventually one or more of your drummers will figure out that they can play both parts at the same time. Be careful not to rush the quarter notes. Ask the whole class to pat the Low Drum and Rattle parts on their thighs; then have the class sing over the top.

2. Teach the Medium Drum part (all high tones on the edge of the drumhead) by having all the students use their dominant hand to pat quarter notes on their thigh. Then add the other hand as in: "R R-L R R-L R R-L R R" (or the reverse). The pattern for the second half of the melody is just like the rhythm of the melody (R R-L R R). Play the Medium Drum part with the recording.

3. Combine both drum parts and rattle along with the recording, singing, and recorders.

Option: Play the drum and rattle parts along with the recording of Mercedes Sosa's "Sólo le Pido a Dios" (see Cultural Connections).

Guitar, Charango (Ukulele) and Bass Parts

These parts are found on the enclosed enhanced audio CD. The Rhythm Guitar 3 part is written to be finger-picked (p=thumb, i=index, m=middle, a=ring), but it can also just be strummed. The Charango part can easily be played on a ukulele. Note the up/down strum patterns for the first and second halves of the melody. The Guitar 1 and 2 parts are available if players can be found who can read in 7th position, or these parts can be played on other instruments (note: the guitar sounds an octave lower than written). Add the easy bass part if a player is available.

Combining All Parts

Put together all of the instruments, players and singers, and then play and sing with the recording. Option: "El Humahuaqueño" may be paired with "In the High Andes" for recorders and World Music Drum Ensemble found in Will Schmid's *More New Ensembles and Songs*, p. 24, book/CD HL 09971087.

Cross-Cultural Connections

If time permits, study some of these connections to the same region of Argentina and Bolivia. You can download other recordings of "El Humahuaqueño" by doing a search for these titles: Santiago y Sus Flautas de Pan, Latin Panpipes & Flutes, Los Koyas, Le top des Andes.

Mercedes Sosa (1935-2009), known as "La Negra" was one of the greatest Argentine singers of all time. Her birthplace, San Miguel de Tecumán, in northwest Argentina, and her European and Amerindian ancestry, made her into a foremost interpreter of Argentine folk and popular music. Mercedes Sosa also fought for social justice and was forced to live outside Argentina for some years. Research and share some of her recordings.

4 Projectable & Printable PDFs on CD
Charango • Drum Ensemble
Guitars • Recorders

Continued from page 14

About Karen Schooley

Co-author of "The Czech-Mex Polka" article, Karen Schooley, is the Music Coordinator at Berlin Metropolitan School, Germany, where she teaches general music classes and directs the BMS Choir. BMS is an International Baccalaureate (IB) World School. It offers the IB Primary Years Program, the Cambridge IGCSE diploma (certificate) and as the school grows and the current ninth grade class (now the oldest students in the school) progress, the school will offer the IB Diploma as well. Karen is a violist, fiddler, and has a passion for both classical orchestra and folk music (especially Irish).

EL HUMAHUAQUEÑO

VOICE 1 *(top & bottom notes,*
in either octave)
VOICE 2 *(middle notes)*

(3 measure introduction)
In a lively 2 ($\quad$ = 80)

Traditional Song from Argentina and Bolivia
Arranged by WILL SCHMID

The original purchaser has permission to reproduce this music for educational use only. Any other use is strictly prohibited.

CHRISTMAS JIG
LESSON PLAN BY WILL SCHMID

The jig is a 6/8 dance popular in Ireland and the British Isles. The Irish frame drum called the Bodhran (BAHW-rahn) (see Cultural Connections) is played with a double-ended stick. The World Music Drum Ensemble for this piece simulates the sound of the Bodhran.

LEARNING SEQUENCE

1. Locate Ireland and the United Kingdom on a map of Europe.

2. Teach the Low Drum and Tambourine parts that accompany both the singing and the instrumental sections. Teach the Medium Drum part on thighs and then drums; then put the Drum Ensemble together.

3. Teach the song, "I Saw Three Ships."

4. Teach the song, "Here We Come a-Wassailing."

5. Teach the Xylophone parts.

6. Combine all these parts with the recording.

LEARNING THE DRUM ENSEMBLE

This World Music Drum Ensemble has only three parts, and the Low Drum and Tambourine play the same rhythm. See bottom of page 21.

1. Teach students to play the Low Drum and Tambourine rhythm on their thighs. Point out that this rhythm is often used as a basic marching cadence. At this point you have the option of teaching students one of the songs, having them do this basic rhythm as they sing. Or, you may choose to go on and teach the Medium Drum part.

2. The Medium Drum part is a typical jig rhythm that is often played on the Irish Bodhran. Teach the first four measures of this part orally using these syllables:

   "Deedle dee dum, Deedle dee dum, Dum dee deedle dee Dum dee dum"

Then have students play the part while continuing to say the syllables. Don't worry about the right/left hand indications until they have the rhythm down. Remind them of the **Drum Rule: If you say the rhythm while you play, you will learn it twice as fast and remember it twice as long.** Then teach them the last four measures (say the same rhythm up to the second-to-the-last "Dum") and put it all together.

3. Combine all of the Drum Ensemble parts and play with the full performance recording (CD track 6).

4. A fun option is to play the drum parts with sticks on the hard shell of the drum. Warning: This can be loud.

SINGING

1. "I Saw Three Ships" is a traditional British Isles Christmas song in call and response form. Teach everyone to sing the melody first; then, if time permits, teach the harmony Voice 2 part which sings only on the response. Consider asking the audience to sing the melody on the responses if the song is used for a program. Additional verses are available in many Christmas songbooks.

2. "Here We Come a-Wassailing" is also a 6/8 British Isles Christmas song. Wassailing songs were used both to toast the apple trees in hopes of a good harvest, (*Here's to thee, old apple tree, That blooms well, bears well. Hats full, caps full, Three bushel bags full, An' all under one tree. Hurrah! Hurrah!*) and as part of the tradition of caroling from house to house at Christmas time. Explain that wassail is a type of apple cider. Teach students this song.

3. Part of the fun of "Here We Come a-Wassailing" is that the song changes meter from 6/8 to 2/4 keeping the beat steady. This should not pose a problem for students, since the underlying drum ensemble parts are only basic. Have half the class pat on their thighs: four measures of 6/8 triplets followed by four measures of even 2/4 eighth notes, while the other half claps the Low Drum/Tambourine part. Then switch parts.

4. When students are ready, sing both songs along with the recording (full performance, CD track 6, accompaniment, CD track 18) and/or the Low Drum and Tambourine parts.

XYLOPHONES

1. The Bass Xylophone and Alto Xylophone 2 parts work together along with the Low Drum and Tambourine rhythm. Although the keys for the songs change from F to C and back, neither of these parts plays either a B or B♭ note, so that bar may be removed.

2. The Soprano Xylophone needs a B♭ bar for "I Saw Three Ships," but "Here We Come a-Wassailing" does not use a B-bar, so no changes need to be made from song to song.

3. The Alto Xylophone 1 part should set up with a regular B-bar, because "I Saw Three Ships" (key of F) does not play the B♭ note. This will allow the instrument to be ready to play "Here We Come a-Wassailing" in the key of C.

4. Combine parts with other instruments and voices when ready.

GUITAR AND BASS

The Guitar part should use a capo placed at fret 3. The Guitar chords are written in the keys of D (capo 3: sounds F) and A (capo 3: sounds C). The chords are plucked at the same time when singing (*p*=thumb, *i*=index, *m*=middle, *a*=ring) and played in a 6/8 pattern (*p-i-am-i*) during instrumentals. The Bass part may be played on any form of string bass or electric bass.

CROSS-CULTURAL CONNECTIONS

The bodhran is the principal Irish drum used for dances. It uses a double-ended stick.

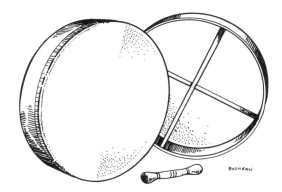

If Irish dancers are available in your community, you might invite them to dance on the instrumental sections of this piece.

The call and response form used in "I Saw Three Ships" can be found in other British Isles ballads such as "Scarborough Fair" or the "Wee Cooper of Fife." It is also a common form in these musical traditions:

- African-American spirituals, work songs and gospel
- Sea shanties
- Jazz and Blues
- Military cadence songs
- West African music
- Caribbean songs

For a more complex workout with Irish drum rhythms, play "Lord of the Bodhran Dance" from World Music Drumming: *More New Ensembles and Songs*, p. 10, HL 09971087.

3 Projectable & Printable PDFs on CD
Drum Ensemble • Guitar/Bass
Xylophones

Drum Ensemble

* Hands: R = Right, L = Left; hands may be switched.

CHRISTMAS JIG

I Saw Three Ships
18th Century English Carol
Here We Come A-Wassailing
Traditional English Carol
Arranged by WILL SCHMID

Lyrics:

I saw three ships come sail-ing in, on Christ-mas Day, on Christ-mas Day. I saw three ships come sail-ing in on Christ-mas Day in the morn-ing.

all the bells on earth shall ring on Christ-mas Day, on Christ-mas Day. And all the bells on earth shall ring on Christ-mas Day in the morn-ing.

And

Here we come a-was-sail-ing a-mong the leaves so green,
are not dai-ly beg-gars that beg from door to door,

Here we come a wan-d'ring, so fair to be seen:
We are neigh-bors' chil-dren whom you have seen be-fore: } Love and joy come to

you, and to you your was-sail too, And God bless you and send you a hap-py New

Year, and God send you a hap-py New Year.

We — let us all re - joice a - gain, on Christ - mas Day, on Christ - mas Day, Then

let us all re - joice a - gain, on Christ - mas Day in the morn - ing. I

saw three ships come sail - ing in, on Christ - mas Day, on Christ - mas Day, I

saw three ships come sail - ing in on Christ - mas Day in the morn - ing.

DULCES SUEÑOS
(SWEET DREAMS)

LESSON PLAN BY WILL SCHMID

In this lesson, we visit the West Coast of Mexico and a little town called La Manzanilla, Jalisco, *(Lah Mahn-zan-EE-ya, Hal-EES-coh)* on the bay known as the Costa Alegre *(COH-stah-LEH-greh)* — the cheerful or happy coast. The Spanish words *Dulces Sueños (DOOL-sehs Soo-EHN-yos)* mean sweet dreams. "Dulces Sueños" is a *mariachi (mah-ree-AH-chee)* serenade that highlights the 2-against-3 rhythms that are a big part of Mexican music.

LEARNING SEQUENCE

1. Teach the chorus to the song, "Dulces Sueños," and learn the meaning and pronunciation of the Spanish words. Sing with the recording.

2. Learn the verses that describe various foods found on the beach. Sing along with the recording (CD track 7).

3. Learn the basic timeline for "Dulces Sueños" and the three parts to the World Music Drum ensemble. Play with the recording.

4. If possible add parts from the mariachi string ensemble: 2 violins, *vihuela (bee-oo-EH-lah)* which may be played on ukulele, 3 guitar parts, and *guitarrón (gee-tahr-OHN),* the Mexican bass guitar. These parts are found on the enclosed enhanced audio CD.

Copyright Emma dusepo @ Wikipedia

LEARNING THE SONG, "DULCES SUEÑOS"

1. The song has a number of Spanish words throughout. Practice the pronunciation and discuss the meaning as follows. If you sing the words on the pitch of the songs, students will learn both the words and the melody at the same time. If students in your class speak Spanish, use them as teacher helpers.

> *Dulces sueños (DOOL-sehs soo-EHN-yos)* = sweet dreams
>
> *buenas noches (boo-EHN-ahs NOH-chehs)* = goodnight
>
> *Costa alegre (elide the two words as COH-stah-LEH-greh)* = happy (cheerful) coast
>
> *playa blanca (PLAH-yah BLAHN-cah)* = white beach
>
> *Mi hamaca (mee ah-MAH-cah)* = my hammock
>
> *churros (CHOOR-rohs)* = a deep-fried pastry a little like a funnel cake
>
> *agua de coco (AH-gwuh deh COH-coh)* = coconut water
>
> *Palateria (pah-lah-tehr-EE-ya)* = ice cream vendor or store
>
> *mango (MAHN-goh)* = a sweet orange fruit sometimes sold on a stick
>
> *piña (PEEN-yah)* = pineapple

2. Practice the 2-against-3 timeline rhythm that alternates measures:

Pat even eighth notes on thighs (left and right hands may be reversed):

LEFT-right-right **LEFT**-right-right / **LEFT**-right **LEFT**-right **LEFT**-right

Then put a rattle in the **LEFT** hand while patting the whole pattern. Follow that by having half the class pat the whole pattern while the other half claps only the **LEFT** hand beats. Then finish by clapping only the first three **LEFT**-hand claps and play along with the recording. Point out that this is the Maracas pattern and continues throughout the piece. Make the connection to "America" from *West Side Story* by Leonard Bernstein.

3. Sing the melody of the Chorus along with the recording; then add the melody for the verses. If time and readiness allow, add the harmony Voice 2 part. Show students how often Mexican and other Latin American songs often have harmony that is a 3rd or a 6th (the inversion of the 3rd) above or below the melody.

LEARNING THE WORLD MUSIC DRUM PARTS

1. The Maracas part (the timeline already learned) may be played with any type of rattle. Play both maracas at once to make it louder. If a shekere-type rattle is used, hit it against a hand or thigh.

2. The Tamborita *(tahm-boh-REE-tah),* literally "little drum," should be played with a padded mallet, and it plays the same timeline as the Maracas.

3. The Conga part may be played on any medium or low drum such as a Tubano. Notice that the right hand (rights and lefts may be reversed) plays in the middle of the drumhead (notehead below the line) on the first beat of each measure. It fills out the timeline. You could have students just play along with the timeline with their right hands to find the important beats; then fill in the rest of the pattern.

4. When the three parts can play together, play along with the recording.

PUTTING IT ALL TOGETHER

You may decide to just have students concentrate on singing one or both of the voice parts and have them sing along with the full recording or accompaniment. Another option would be to add some of the instrument parts (depending on what is available) in an order something like this.

1. Maracas, Tamborita, Conga.

2. Guitar 3 may play the finger-style arrangement or just follow the chords by strumming the rhythm.

3. Guitarrón (Mexican bass guitar; see photo on p. 24) may be played on any bass stringed instrument.

4. Vihuela may also be played on the ukulele.

5. Violins 1 and 2, Guitars 1 and 2 may be added if available.

The Piano part is primarily for rehearsal purposes.

CULTURAL CONNECTIONS

- Show photos of Mexican beach scenes, musicians, and foods mentioned in the song. If Mexican heritage students are in your class, have them discuss some of their favorite Mexican foods.

- Listen to recordings of mariachi music by going to iTunes and searching for "mariachi."

3 Projectable & Printable PDFs on CD
Drum Ensemble • Guitars • Violins

Drum Ensemble

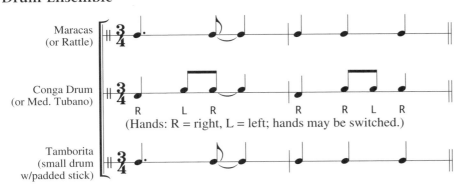

DULCES SUEÑOS
(SWEET DREAMS)

Words and Music by
WILL SCHMID

Mariachi Serenade (♩ = 132)

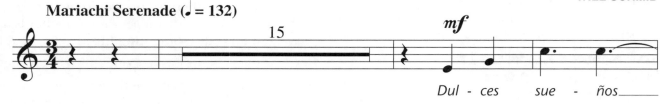

Dul - ces sue - ños____

____ buen - as no - ches, may your dreams be sweet ev - 'ry

night. Cos - ta a_le - gre,____ pla - ya blan - ca

on the sands be - neath the moon - light. Mi ha -

ma - ca____ oh how com - fy, it swings light - ly____

____ in the breeze, Dul - ces sue - ños,____ buen - as

no - ches, may your dreams be sweet ev - 'ry night.

Day - time we head to the beach where the

84 wa - gons of sweets are ped - dling their wares.

89 Cin - na - mon chur - ros and *ag - ua de co - co* are tempt - ing our

Part I *mf*

Part II

94 eyes as we stare. *Dul - ces sue - ños,_____ buen - as*

99 *no - ches,* may your dreams be sweet ev - 'ry night.

104 *Cos - ta a_le - gre,_____ pla - ya blan - ca,* on the

109 sands be - neath the moon - light. *Mi ha - ma - ca,_____*

114 ___ oh how com - fy, it swings light - ly_____ in the

119 breeze, *Dul - ces sue - ños,_____ buen - as no - ches,* may your

33

125 dreams be sweet ev - 'ry night.

HANA KUPONO

LESSON PLAN BY WILL SCHMID AND MAREN OOM

Kuma Pua Garmon

"Hana Kupono" is a Hawaiian chant (*oli*) composed by **Kumu Pua Garmon**: "It uses *'Olelo No'eau: Hawaiian Proverbs and Poetical Sayings* (Mary Kawena Puku'i. Bishop Museum Press, 1983). These Proverbs were arranged by me to put it in a chant form. The purpose is that the child, student or adult chants this in hopes to become that person or student or to reinforce who they are becoming — someone who works honestly, who is alert, who stand firms, who is proud, who is strong in mind and body, and finally famous are the flowers (children) of Hawaii nei."

Maren Oom

Maren Oom, collaborator for this lesson and arrangement, is Chair of the Arts at St. Mary's International Baccalaureate World School, Aliso Viejo, CA. Prior to that she was Director of Fine Arts at Parker School, Kamuela, HI. Maren has extensive experience in music, dance, and theatre and holds a M.A., University of Hawaii-Manoa and a B.F.A. from Emerson College, Boston, MA.

LEARNING SEQUENCE

1. Locate Hawaii on a map and learn the names of the Islands. Discuss Hawaiian history and culture.

2. Teach the two-note chant for *"Hana Kupono."*

3. Teach the drum and Ipu (gourd) parts to the World Music Drum Ensemble.

4. Teach the high and low stick parts for the instrumental interlude.

5. Teach the optional guitar and ukulele parts found on the enclosed enhanced CD.

6. Combine all these parts with the recording.

ABOUT HAWAII

Hawaii is the most recent (1959) of the fifty United States to join the union. It is composed of eight main islands (from SE to NW: Hawai'i (Big Island), Maui, Kaho'olawe, Lana'i, Moloka'i, O'ahu, Kaua'i, and Ni'ihau), and its capitol city is Honolulu. Search "Hawaii" on the Internet and learn more about its history and culture.

SINGING THE CHANT

Start by discussing the meaning of the chant and its hope for the future of each student. See the translation of each line below. It might be interesting for students to make a poster with these proverbs on it. Then teach everyone how to sing and pronounce the Hawaiian words to "Hana Kupono" one phrase at a time. It is best to learn how to pronounce the words by singing rather than separating the words and pitches. Hawaiians sing with a relaxed and open-throated sound. The low-to-medium pitches for the song were chosen to achieve that effect.

Hana kupono kakou (Hah-nah koo-poh-noh kah-koh) = We work honestly.

E maka'ala kakou (Ay mah-kah-ah-lah kah-koh) = We are alert.

Ku ha'aheo kakou (Koo hah-ah-hay-oh kah-koh) = We are proud.

E 'onipa'a kakou (Ay oh-nee-pah-ah kah-koh) = We stand firm.

Ikaika ka mana'o me ke kino (Ee-kayee-kah kah mah-nah-oh may kay kee-noh) = Be strong in mind and body.

Kulia loa'a ka na'auao (Koo-lee-ah loh-ah-ah kah nah-auoo-aow) = Strive to obtain wisdom.

Kaulana na pua o Hawai'i nei (Kauoo-lah-nah nah pooah oh Hah-vah-ee nayee) = Famous are the flowers (children) of Hawai'i nei (our Hawaii)

When everyone knows the melody and words, try chanting it along with the full performance recording (CD track 8).

LEARNING THE DRUM ENSEMBLE

The **Medium Drum** may be played on a Tubano or other conga-type drum. Play all notes below the line as "low" tones in the center of the drumhead. "High" tones, notes above the line, are played on the edge of the drumhead. Note the right-hand and left-hand indications. The R and L hands may be reversed by any player. Practice saying: "Low Low-high Low (off)"; then put the pattern on the drum.

The **Ipu Gourd** part may be played on the butt of a large hollow gourd, an end of a large plastic bottle, or even on a desktop. The two basic Ipu sounds are:

U (oo) is a low resonant tone played with the heel of the hand.

Te (tay) is a high sound played with the fingertips.

Consult the Internet for a video demonstration. Type "Hawaiian Drum Instruments Ipu" in your preferred search engine and find one that suits your needs. The *Ipu* part may be simplified by playing quarter notes on beats 1 and 2 as follows:

U U U-Te Te (Heel Heel Heel-Tip Tip)

The full part notated below is:

U -Te U-Te U-Te Te (Heel-Tip Heel-Tip Heel-Tip Tip)

The **High and Low Stick** parts are meant to be played on any pieces of wood that can produce two different pitches. Either dowels or drumsticks will work here. Practice the complementary rhythms; then combine with the Medium Drum and Ipu. The Sticks play only on the instrumental interlude between chanting.

OPTIONAL GUITAR & UKULELE

The Guitar part is strummed using only an Am chord with a capo at fret 2 (sounds Bm). Dampen the strings (x-notes played with either the side of the thumb or palm) on beat 2 and 4 to produce a more rhythmic effect.

Strum pattern for Ukulele
Down-Up-Up Down Down-Up

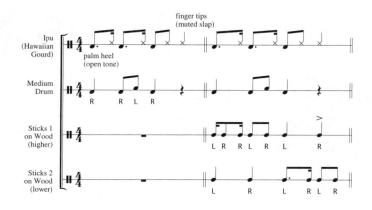

CROSS-CULTURAL CONNECTIONS

Ideas for cross-cultural connections are available on the enclosed enhanced CD.

5 Projectable & Printable PDFs on CD
Connections • Drum Ensemble
Guitar • Ukulele • Vocals

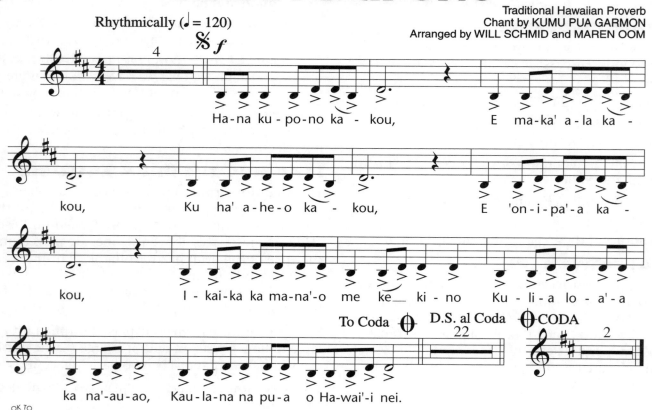

HANA KUPONO

Traditional Hawaiian Proverb
Chant by KUMU PUA GARMON
Arranged by WILL SCHMID and MAREN OOM

Rhythmically (♩ = 120)

Ha-na ku-po-no ka - kou,   E ma-ka' a-la ka -

kou,   Ku ha' a-he-o ka - kou,   E 'on-i-pa'-a ka -

kou,   I - kai-ka ka ma-na'-o me ke__ ki-no Ku-li-a lo-a'-a

To Coda   D.S. al Coda   CODA

ka na'-au-ao, Kau-la-na na pu-a o Ha-wai'-i nei.

SALMA YA SAALEMA

LESSON PLAN BY WILL SCHMID AND REBECCA NERENHAUSEN

This Arabic work song from Egypt comes to us by way of Rebecca Nerenhausen who teaches elementary music in Cairo, Egypt. The song was popularized by Egyptian composer, Sheikh Sayed Darwish. In the early twentieth century, Darwish wrote songs for the common worker and songs to promote Egyptian nationalism, such as "Bilaadii, Bilaadii," Egypt's national anthem. He wrote verses to accompany "Salma Ya Saalema," which people sang when going off on a dangerous mission, such as work on the Suez Canal.

LEARNING SEQUENCE

1. Find Cairo, Egypt, and the Suez Canal on a map

2. Learn the melody and Arabic lyrics of the Refrain to the song, "Salma Ya Saalema." Add the harmony voice part if students are at that level.

3. Learn the two drum parts and tambourine part. Put them together with the singing.

4. Add the solo if Arabic speakers are available. Otherwise these solo parts are available on the recording.

5. Study Cultural Connections as your progress and time permits.

LEARNING THE SONG, "SALMA YA SAALEMA"

1. Begin by orally teaching students the Arabic words and melody to the Refrain.

   Pronunciation of the refrain words according to the *Dictionary of the Spoken Arabic* of Cairo is:

   Sal-ma ya saa-le-ma = *Sahl-mah yah sal-leh-mah*

   Rokh-na w'gee-na = *rohch*-nah wih-gay-nah*

   bil saa-le-ma = *bill sal-leh-mah*

   *The kh is like a "clearing the throat" sound as in the German "Bach."

   Although the pronunciation of the Arabic may present a challenge, time spent on this is a major step toward cultural understanding. Display Arabic Text below, and point out that Arabic (like Hebrew) is read from right to left (not left to right as in European languages). The translation of the refrain is:

"We left in peace, and we returned in peace."

سللة ياسلامة رحنا وجينا بالسلامة

2. Teach the skeleton melody and pronunciation as follows by having students echo.

3. Now combine these sections to sing the whole skeleton melody of the Refrain.

4. Once students can sing the skeleton melody and words with ease, teach them the complete ornamented melody in Voice 2. Explain that Arabic melodies are full of **ornaments** — notes that weave around the skeleton melody. (See Cultural Connections)

5. When students have learned the Voice 2 melody to the Refrain, you may wish to add the Voice 1 part that includes a higher part on the second and fourth phrases.

6. The Solo or Soli part for the Verse (repeated) could be sung by students / or community adults proficient in Arabic or left to be performed by the recording. During the verse students should hum quietly on the drone note G (notice the drone G notes in both the Piano and the Oud 3 (Guitar 3) parts. The translation of the verse is:

"The whistle blew for the train to stop and left me in this city.

Not America, not Europe … There is no better town than mine."

LEARNING THE WORLD MUSIC DRUM PARTS

1. Begin by teaching the Tambourine and Low Frame Drum parts below.

2. Then teach the Egyptian Tabla (Doumbek) part in any of its versions from easy (1) to more complex (4). This part may be played on any drum that has both a low and a high tone. The

goblet-shaped drums like the Middle Eastern *doumbek* or *darabuka* will sound best, or the goblet-shaped *djembe* may also be used. Notes below the line are bass tones played in the middle of the drumhead. Notes above the line are played at the edge of the head.

3. Combine parts and play along with the full performance (CD track 9).

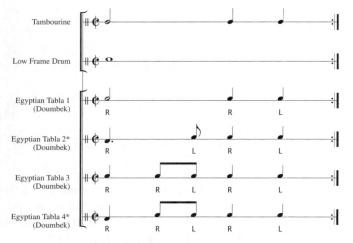

* Play Tabla Part 2 or 4 if possible. Tabla Parts 1 & 3 are skeleton parts.

ACCOMPANYING WITH OUD (GUITAR) AND SANTOOR (PIANO)

All of the Oud (*lute*) parts may be played on guitar. The Middle Eastern *Santoor* is a hammered dulcimer and may be played on the piano (also a type of hammered dulcimer where the hammers are triggered by depressing keys instead of hammering directly on the strings. These parts are available on the enclosed enhanced CD.

COMBINING ALL PARTS

Put together all of the parts with whatever instruments are available. Sing and play along with the full recording (CD track 9 or just the accompaniment CD track 21).

CROSS-CULTURAL CONNECTIONS

If time permits, study some of these instruments found in Egypt; photos, video and audio sources can be easily found on the Internet.

- **Egyptian Tabla** *[Tab-LAH]* is a goblet-shaped drum better known as either a **Doumbek** *[DOOM-bek]* or *Darabuka [Dahr-a-BOO-ka]*. The Egyptian *Tabla* should not be confused with the Indian *Tabla* (two pot-shaped drums) often heard with the Indian *Sitar*.

- **Oud** *[OOD]* is a Middle Eastern name for the pear-shaped lute.

- **Santoor** *[Sahn-TOOR]* sometimes spelled *Santur* is a hammered dulcimer (strings stretched across a flat box) that is played with handheld wooden hammers.

Some elements of Middle Eastern music are quite different from the music of Europe or America:

- **Melody** is highly embellished with extra notes and is the most important element. Other places to find highly embellished singing is in African-American pop singers such as Whitney Houston or Michael Jackson or in Baroque opera or oratorio.

- **Harmony** (except for modern western-influenced music) is largely non-existent. Chords are not used in traditional music. Drones (single sustained notes) may be used to underpin the melody.

- **Instruments** such as the *Oud* and *Santoor* usually play the melody, often in a highly embellished manner.

The Putumayo album, Arabic Groove (PUT 189-2), has an interesting mix of contemporary Arabic music. The song, "Hely Meli," works well with the Drum Ensemble from this lesson. Numerous pop versions of "Salma Ya Saalema" (sometimes spelled "Salma Ya Salama") are available on both iTunes and on YouTube (pre-screen for belly dancers). Most of the pop versions have a different verse and use Western chord sequences, but the refrain sounds more traditional.

CAIRO, EGYPT

- Go to the Internet and do a Google search for "Cairo, Egypt;" then do another search for "Suez Canal."

- Music teacher and co-author of this article, **Rebecca Nerenhausen**, teaches elementary music at Cairo American College, a pre K–12 International Baccalaureate coeducational day school of approximately 1,200 students (569 U.S. citizens, 177 host-country nationals, and 444 other nationalities).

Rebecca Nerenhausen in Cairo classroom.

3 Projectable & Printable PDFs on CD
Drum Ensemble • Oud • Piano

SALMA YA SAALEMA

Sayed Darwish
Arranged by WILL SCHMID
and REBECCA NERENHAUSEN

GLOBAL GROOVES

SAMIOTISA

LESSON PLAN BY WILL SCHMID AND DEBBIE DEGENHARDT

The dance music of Greece is often written in 7/8 meter and is danced in lines or circles rather than couples. "Samiotisa" is a well-known Greek dance song from the Island of Samos.

LEARNING SEQUENCE

1. Locate Greece on a map and share some photos from the beautiful Greek islands by typing "photos Greek islands" in your preferred search engine.

2. Teach the 7/8 meter used in "Samiotisa" and learn to play the World Music Drum Ensemble parts along with the recording.

3. Teach the song, "Samiotisa" in both Greek and English.

4. Add any of the instrumental parts that are playable.

5. Combine all these with the recording, first the full performance (CD track 10) and then the accompaniment recording (CD track 22).

LEARNING THE 7/8 DRUM ENSEMBLE

This World Music Drum Ensemble has three parts, and one, two, or all three can be played while singing "Samiotisa." The 7/8 meter is really felt as 3 beats (also conducted in 3), one of which is slightly longer. The 7 subdivisions are commonly grouped as 3-2-2 (as in "Samiotisa") or 2-2-3.

1. Ask students to pat the following pattern on their thighs saying the numbers aloud (The Left and Right hands may be reversed):

1	2	3	1	2	1	2
L	R	R	L	R	L	R

2. When students can do this with confidence, put tambourines (or rattles) in the left hands of your most competent players. Have them play the tambourine on all of the left hands while continuing to pat the right-hand subdivisions. Have the whole class play (pat) along with the recording (CD track 10).

3. Now show students how their subdivisions can be played on a drum using Low (middle of the drumhead) and High (edge of the drumhead) tones. This is the pattern intended for the goblet-shaped drum known as a *Doumbek* (DOOM-bek), named after its two sounds: the low "doom" and the high "bek" or "tek." This drum is played throughout the Middle East and North Africa.

1	2	3	1	2	1	2
Low	High	High	Low	High	Low	High

Those students not on a drum can pat the rhythm on their thighs.

4. When ready, combine this with tambourines and play lightly with the recording. There is a small variation on this part that may be played by one or two of your best players. The variation should only be played sparingly during measures of the song that have long notes. The Doumbek variation is played by rolling these fingers: ring (r), middle (m), index (i).

1	2 & 3	1	2	1	2
Low	r m i	Low	High	Low	High

5. The Low Drum part may be the most difficult to master, because the player has to feel all of the hidden subdivisions. The Greeks play this part on the two-headed Daouli (DAH-oh-oo-lee) with a heavy stick (Daouli Stick) on one head and a long, thin stick on the other. Have students first pat this part on their thighs; then put it on any single-headed drum with either heavy stick or a hand on the head and the thin stick hitting the side of the drum shell. Say the subdivisions out loud, hitting where indicated. Notice that 3 of these hits coincide with the Tambourine.

1	2	3	1	2	1	2
Head		Side	Head		Side	

Watch students' hands to see who is ready to play this pattern on the drum.

6. Play all parts with the recording when ready.

SINGING

The melody to "Samiotisa" will be easier to sing after playing the Drum Ensemble parts along with the recording.

Start by having students echo you on the first two measures (Samiotisa = Sah-meeOH-tee-sah) while lightly playing or tapping the tambourine part. Then sing the rest of the phrase on a neutral syllable like "da" or "la." Combine the word "Samiotisa" and the syllables and practice the first phrase. When ready teach the second phrase using neutral syllables. If students can hear the skeleton tones Sol, Re, Mi, and Do at the beginning of each measure, it will make it easier to learn. Sing the whole melody along with the recording.

The pronunciation for the Greek words in the first and last verse is:

Samiotisa = Sah-meeOH-tee-sah

Pote tha pas sti Samo =
   Poh-teh thah pahs stee Sah-moh

Roda tha rixo sto yia lo Samiotisa =
   Roh-dah thah ree-ksoh stoh yah loh Sah-meeoh-tee-sah

Roda tha rixo sto yia na 'rtho na se paro =
   Roh-dah thah ree-ksoh stoh yah nah rthoh nah seh pah-roh

The English translation is found in paraphrased form in verse two.

Here are some singing options (from easiest/quickest to most complete):

- Sing the complete song in 1 or 2 parts on neutral syllable and/or English.
- Sing the first phrase in Greek and the second phrase on neutral syllables.
- Sing the complete arrangement in Greek and English w/Tambourine.
- Sing all and play 2 or 3 of the World Music Drum Ensemble parts.

OPTIONAL OTHER PARTS

- The *Bouzouki* (may be played on steel-string guitars or mandolins), guitar, bass, violin, and Bb clarinet parts are available as PDFs on the enclosed enhanced CD.

EXTENSIONS FOR SAMIOTISA

For more about "Samiotisa, there is a PDF on the enclosed enhanced CD that includes a dance activity and cross-cultural connections.

6 Projectable & Printable PDFs on CD
Bouzouki • Clarinet • Drum Ensemble
Extensions • Guitar/Bass • Lyra (Violin)

Drum Ensemble

* Right hand holding a heavy Daouli Stick or use hand in middle of head for a bass tone. Greek drum is 2-headed field drum.
** Left hand plays a light thin stick on the shell of the drum.

Co-author of this article, Debbie Degenhardt, has been a public school music teacher since 1986. She received her Bachelors from SUNY at Fredonia in Music Education and her Masters in Jazz/Commercial Performance from Manhattan School of Music. She has earned her Master Level in Orff-Schulwerk having studied under Carol Huffman, Robert deFrece, Jos Wuytack and Steven Calantropio. Debbie has completed three levels of World Music Drumming. In addition to being a performer, composer/arranger and lyricist, she has taught all grade levels including alternative high school, music therapy, and is presently in a K-5 position in the Sachem, NY School District. Her latest accomplishment is the publication of her Common Core-based songs found in, *Literacy Through Music — a Cross-Curricular Reference* for grades 1 and 2. Her CD recordings of these songs will soon be available soon. Debbie has relatives who come from the Greek Island of Samos.

SAMIOTISA

Traditional Greek Wedding Song
Arranged by WILL SCHMID
and DEBBIE DEGENHARDT

In 3+2+2 (♪ = 240)

Sa - mio - ti - sa, Sa - mio - ti - sa,
mio - ti - sa, Sa - mio - ti - sa,

Po - te tha pas sti Sa - mo?___ Sa - mio - ti - sa, Sa - mio - ti - sa,
When will you go to Sa - mo?___ Sa - mio - ti - sa, Sa - mio - ti - sa,

Po - te tha pas sti Sa - mo?___ Ro - da tha ri - xo sto yia -
When will you go to Sa - mo?___ I will spread ros - es on the

lo Sa - mio - ti - sa yia na - 'rtho na se pa - ro. Ro - da tha ri - xo sto yia -
shore Sa - mio - ti - sa to greet you when you come. I will spread ros - es on the

lo Sa - mio - ti - sa yia na - 'rtho na se pa - ro. Sa -
shore Sa - mio - ti - sa to greet you when you come.

And to the boat you trav - el on, I will add gold - en___

sails.___ And to the boat you trav - el on, I will add gold - en___ sails.___

Gold-en pad-dles I will use, Sa-mio-ti-sa, to come and bring you here to me.

Gold-en pad-dles I will use, Sa-mio-ti-sa, to come and bring you here to me.

Sa - mio - ti - sa, Sa - mio - ti - sa, Po - te tha pas sti Sa -

mo?__ Sa - mio - ti - sa, Sa - mio - ti - sa, Po - te tha pas sti Sa - mo?__

Ro - da tha ri - xo sto yia - lo Sa-mio-ti-sa yia na - 'rtho na se pa - ro.

Ro - da tha ri - xo sto yia - lo Sa-mio-ti-sa yia na - 'rtho na se pa - ro.__

ZANGELEWA

LESSON PLAN BY WILL SCHMID

"Zangelewa (Waka Waka)" is a song from Cameroon, a country on the West Coast of Africa. This "walking song" (waka waka) is a widely sung by school children, sporting clubs, boy scouts, and marching soldiers throughout the continent. In 2010, Shakira's version of the song, "Waka Waka (This Time for Africa)" was the official anthem of the FIFA World Cup Soccer Tournament. "Zangelewa" (zahn-geh-LEH-wah) is often performed in the *highlife* style from Ghana now popular throughout West Africa.

LEARNING SEQUENCE

1. Locate Cameroon on a map of Africa and learn about its history and traditions.

2. Teach the refrain of the song; then teach the verses.

3. Teach the five-part Highlife World Music Drum Ensemble.

4. Teach the optional xylophone parts.

5. Combine all these parts with the recording.

LEARNING THE SONG, "ZANGELEWA (WAKA, WAKA)"

1. First teach everyone how to sing the skeleton melody of the refrain using only the words, "waka waka eh eh" (mm. 17-24). Sing in an accented, detached (non legato) style throughout the song. "Waka" is pidgin English for "walk while working." "Eh" (rhymes with HEY) is just an exclamation and has no meaning.

2. Next have the class echo the key rhythm, melody and words to mm. 29-30, "Zamina mina eh eh"; then teach the rest of the refrain (mm. 29-36).

3. Here is the pronunciation and rough meaning for the lyrics in the Central African language of *Fang*: (This song is often sung without anyone knowing the meaning of the song.)

   Zamina mina *(ZAH-mee-nah mee-nah)* = come

   Waka waka eh eh *(WAH-kuh WAH-kuh eh eh)* = do it (the work), walk

   Zangelewa *(ZAHN-geh-leh-wah)* = Who has called you?

   Anawa ah ah *(AH-nah-wah ah ah)* = Yes, I did

   Jango (JAHN-goh) OR Zambo *(ZAHM-boh)* = wait

4. When the class knows the refrain melody well, add the lower voice harmony part if time permits.

5. The **Solo** sections may be sung by a soloist, a small group or the whole class in unison. Put it all together with the full performance recording (CD track 11) or the accompaniment recording (CD track 23) when students are ready.

LEARNING THE DRUM ENSEMBLE

Teach the 4-5 parts in the following order:

1. The **Low Frame Drum** (large hand drum) plays on all beats of the measure. On beat 1, play a "high" open tone (sounds low) on the edge of the drum; then on beat 2, play a muted tone (x-head) in the center of the drumhead by leaving the hand down. This should sound like "DOOM – dut." You mostly want to hear beat 1.

2. The **High Bell** ("ding") and **Rattle** ("chah") should be taught to work together as follows:

Beats:	1	&	2	&	1	&	2	&	1	2
Say:	(chah)				ding	chah	ding	chah	ding	chah

Have players say the "ding-chah" while patting their thighs R L R L R L (or the reverse) Be sure to start on the "&" of 2 rather than on beat 1. The rattle part is easy because it is on the beat, but the bell part on the upbeat will be easier if the players continue to say the "ding-chah" pattern while playing. Then have them play both parts while saying the lyrics "waka waka eh eh."

- The **Medium Drum** may be played on a Tubano or other conga-type drum. Play all "high" tones on the edge of the drum. Say "dig-ga dum" into beat 1.

- Option: Teachers familiar with the "World Music Drumming Ensemble 3" may add the rattle and cowbell parts from that ensemble to the ensemble on the next page. Tip: the cowbell part fits with the bold syllables of "**Za**–mi–**na** mi–**na** eh eh"

- Play the drum ensemble with the recording (CD tracks 11 and 23).

LEARNING THE XYLOPHONE ENSEMBLE

- Use medium hard rubber mallets to cut through the drum ensemble.

- The "Zamina mina" first measure is the key to these parts. If some players cannot play these measures quickly enough, you could ask them to play a skeleton part by playing only on these bold syllables: "**Za**–mi–**na** mi–**na eh eh**," which is the rhythm played by the Bass Xylophone in measure 1.

- Combine parts with singing and drums.

These parts are available on the enclosed enhanced CD.

OPTIONAL GUITAR, BASS, AND FLUTE PARTS

- An easy way to play the Guitar part on strings 1-3 is to capo at fret 5 and play the following chord substitutions (capo chords in italics):

- G=*D*   D=*A*   D6=*A6* (add 4th finger on string 1, fret 2)   C=*G*   D7=*A7*

- The Flute part adds a countermelody on the last two repeats of the Refrain.

- The Bass part may be played on any kind of acoustic or electric bass.

These parts are available on the enclosed enhanced CD.

CROSS-CULTURAL CONNECTIONS

This song is performed in the same style as "Highlife Christmas" from *Beatbox* book (HL 09971706). Highlife is one of the biggest musical styles to come out of Ghana, West Africa. This style began around the end of World War II in 1945 and continues to be popular today all over West and Central Africa. It is sung and may be played on either acoustic instruments (drums, bells, rattles, guitar, band instruments) or on electric instruments (guitar, bass, synthesizer). Other names for similar African music styles include *Afropop* and *Juju*.

4 Projectable & Printable PDFs on CD
- Drum Ensemble • Flute
Guitar/Bass • Xylophones

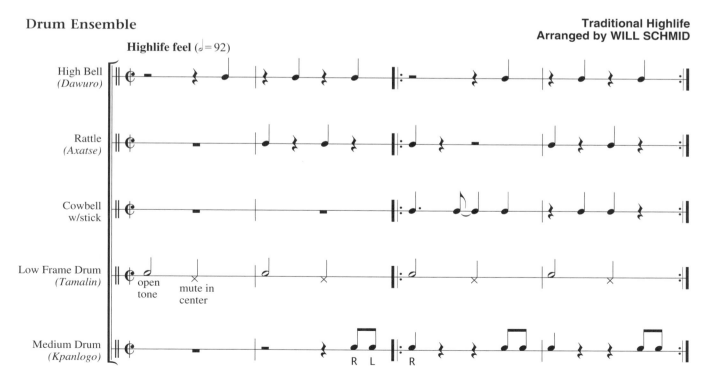

Drum Ensemble

Traditional Highlife
Arranged by WILL SCHMID

ZANGELEWA

Traditional Cameroon
Arranged by WILL SCHMID

Rhythmically (♩ = 92)

DIP AN' FALL BACK
LESSON PLAN BY WILL SCHMID & GILLY HUNTINGTON-RAINEY

"Dip an Fall Back" is a popular West Indian song created around World War II by street musicians. It is a *mento* song (a genre often featuring a 3+3+2 rhythm—the strong half of *clavé*) from Jamaica, also known for *reggae, ska,* and *rocksteady.* "Dip an' Fall Back" comes to us by way of Gilly Huntington-Rainey, music teacher from the Island of Antigua.

LEARNING SEQUENCE

1. Locate Jamaica and Antigua on a map of The Caribbean and learn about their history and traditions.
2. Teach the refrain of the song.
3. Teach the parts to the World Music Drum Ensemble.
4. Teach the verses.
5. Teach the optional xylophone parts.
6. Combine all these parts with the recording and optional guitar and bass parts.

THE ISLANDS OF JAMAICA AND ANTIGUA

On a map, locate Jamaica (south of Cuba) and Antigua (An-TEE-guh) in the Caribbean eastern chain of islands. Both islands were once part of the British Commonwealth, but are now independent. Study the development of Jamaican music styles: reggae, ska, and rocksteady.

SINGING

The melody to the "Dip an' Fall Back" refrain predictably outlines the I, IV, and V chords most of the time. The challenge will be to get students to sing the syncopated rhythms. To help them feel the up-beat syncopations, slow down the tempo so the eighth-note gets the beat; then have them create the subdivision by patting between their thighs and their other hand. Once this "down-up tool" is going, have them sing the first phrase over and over.

Rehearse the third measure of the melody ("My advice there is nutting nice"), which goes up the V

chord and comes down the IV chord, until students can sing it with confidence.

The lyrics to this *mento* song are usually sung in a Jamaican Creole dialect. Here is what Antiguan music teacher, Gilly Huntington-Rainey says about it: "This was probably written during or right after World War II when food, and certainly meat, was scarce. It's called "Dip an(d) Fall Back" because the dish was served in a bowl in the middle of the table and you lean forward to dip your 'boil banana' and then fall back. I'm not sure if that's because you've finished dipping or because it's so delicious! The actual dish is highly seasoned and made from salted fish cooked in coconut milk with all the ingredients that are listed in the song, until it becomes thick and creamy. It is served with starchy root vegetables, known collectively as *'ground provision,'* such as yams and dasheen (a form of taro root) or boiled (green) bananas. Some of the special words in the song are:

Bebridge – a drink made from freshly made cane sugar (mostly molasses) and then mixed with water, lime juice and ice.

Boil banana – green, unripe peeled bananas, which are boiled and eaten as a vegetable

Dray – low open sided cart

Tomatis – tomatoes

The verses may be sung by soloists or sections of singers. Since the song tells a story, the verse singers should emphasize the important words and exercise some freedom with the phrasing.

Once the class can successfully sing the melody, sing along with the full performance recording (CD track 12). Wait with the verses until after learning the World Music Drumming Ensemble parts.

LEARNING THE DRUM ENSEMBLE

This World Music Drum Ensemble has two Drum parts plus Maracas and Guiro parts. The **Low Drum** may be played on a Tubano or other conga-type drum. Play all notes below the line as "low" tones in the center of the drumhead. "High" tones, notes above the line, are played on the edge of the drumhead. Note the right- and left-hand indications. The R and L hands may be reversed by any player. Start by teaching players to play the R hand on all four beats "low low low low;" let the hand fall to the drum head without the usual bounce. Then add the high tone to complete the pattern as "low---high low, low---high low." Play this part and sing the Refrain. The **Bongo Drums** play on the up-beats between the main Low Drum beats. Have students practice tapping the Low Drum main beats on their thighs while saying "high" and "low-low" in between:

 Tap High Tap Low-low Tap   High Tap Low-low

Students may wish to tap the steady beat with one hand while playing the Bongos with the other hand. The Bongos may also be played on a High Drum and a Medium Drum. Put the Bongos and Low Drum parts together. The **Maracas** and the **Guiro** parts are the same traditional patterns found in the *World Music Drumming Curriculum, Ensemble 4* (HL09970094). The Maracas simply alternate hands with a punching motion (no wrist). The Guiro plays a long down (away) stroke followed by two staccato up strokes.

Combine all parts and play with the recording. Add the singing on the Refrain.

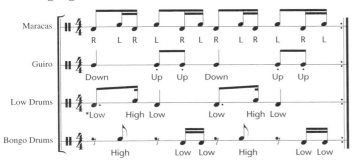

LEARNING THE OPTIONAL XYLOPHONE PARTS (MARIMBAS OR STEEL DRUMS)

The **Soprano Xylophone** (SX) and **Alto Xylophone** (AX) parts are identical and include a number of easy-to-play two-mallet hits. These parts are the same as the Vocal parts 1 and 2 and may be practiced together.

The **Bass Xylophone** (BX) plays the traditional *mento* rhythm (3+3+2; the strong half of *clavé*). It outlines the I, IV, and V chord much of the time. The BX part is similar to the Electric Bass or the Piano Left Hand. If BX players have difficulty with the syncopation, have them practice tapping this pattern on their thighs:

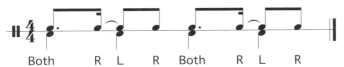

OPTIONAL GUITAR AND BASS PARTS

The Guitar part is written to be played finger-style (p=thumb, i=index, m=middle, a=ring finger), but less experienced players may just strum the chords. Place a capo at fret 5 and play the Guitar Part in the key of G. It will sound in the key of C. The Bass part may be played on any kind of acoustic or electric bass.

NOTE: A piano accompaniment part as well as the optional xylophone, bass, and guitar parts are available as PDFs on the enclosed enhanced CD.

Gilly Huntington-Rainey was an artist and chef before joining Island Academy International School in Antigua where she teaches general music to K-7. Island Academy is a K–13 International Baccalaureate School and has a very diverse student body with children from over 30 different countries and a strong scholarship program to help those less fortunate attend the school.

She is the director of The Island Academy Chamber Choir and Island Marimba. Gilly has lived and worked in Antigua for the past 30 years, having arrived on the island on a yacht in 1983. Gilly believes passionately in the power and importance of music in education and that, along with love, it is the single greatest gift we can give our children. She never misses an opportunity for the children to perform and is dedicated to the ideals of peace and unity through music. She is married with 3 beautiful boys who are all musicians.

Junior Guitar Club

4 Projectable & Printable PDFs on CD
Guitar/Bass • Drum Ensemble
Piano • Xylophones

DIP AN' FALL BACK

**Traditional Jamaican Mento
Arranged by WILL SCHMID
and GILLY HUNTINGTON-RAINEY**

Rhythmically with accent and space (♩ = 92)

REFRAIN
mf

Dip an fall __ back,   dip an fall __ back,

cont. sim.

My ad-vice __ there is nut-ting nice __ like de dip an fall __ back.   Dip an fall __ back,

dip an fall __ back,   My ad-vice __ there is nut-ting nice __ like de dip an fall __ back.

Verse 1 (solo or small group)

An when de war was o - ver __ an ev - 'ry-ting __ was scarce,   An

man was 'xper-i-ment -ing wid tings to fill dem space.   We had a lot __ of food but __ de

meat was out a stock,   So to get a blend, we re-com-mend de dip an fall __ back.

REFRAIN
f

Dip an fall __ back,   dip an fall __ back,   My ad-vice __ there is nut-ting nice __ like de

ABOUT THE ENCLOSED
ENHANCED CD

This CD can be played in a regular CD player or through your computer, and includes audio songs tracks (with and without singers) and PDFs of all the instrument parts and some lesson extensions.

AUDIO DEMONSTRATION TRACKS (WITH VOCALS)

1. In Havana
2. Wewe Ni Mungu Wetu
3. Domidow
4. The Czech-Mex Polka
5. El Humahuaqueño
6. Christmas Jig
7. Dulces Sueños
8. Hana Kupono
9. Salma Ya Saalema
10. Samiotisa
11. Zangelewa
12. Dip an' Fall Back

AUDIO ACCOMPANIMENT TRACKS

13. In Havana
14. Wewe Ni Mungu Wetu
15. Domidow
16. The Czech-Mex Polka
17. El Humahuaqueño
18. Christmas Jig
19. Dulces Sueños
20. Hana Kupono
21. Salma Ya Saalema
22. Samiotisa
23. Zangelewa
24. Dip an' Fall Back

CONTENTS OF PDF FOLDER:

projectable & printable instrument parts, and some lesson extensions

In Havana
3 PDFs: Drum Ensemble, Guitar/Bass, Piano

Wewe Ni Mungu Wetu
5 PDFs: Guitar/Bass, Drum Ensemble, Piano, Recorders, Full Vocals

Domidow
3 PDFs: Drum Ensemble, Mallets, Piano

The Czech-Mex Polka
6 PDFs: Accordion, Clarinet, Drum Ensemble, Trombone, Trumpets, Tuba

El Humahuaqueño
4 PDFs: Charango, Drum Ensemble, Guitars, Recorders

Christmas Jig
3 PDFs: Drum Ensemble, Guitar/Bass, Xylophones

Dulces Sueños
3 PDFs: Drum Ensemble, Guitars, Violins

Hana Kupono
5 PDFs: Connections, Drum Ensemble, Guitar, Ukulele, Vocals

Salma Ya Saalema
3 PDFs: Drum Ensemble, Oud, Piano

Samiotisa
6 PDFs: Bouzouki, Clarinet, Drum Ensemble, Extensions, Guitar/Bass, Lyra (Violin)

Zangelewa
4 PDFs: Drum Ensemble, Flute, Guitar/Bass, Xylophones

Dip an' Fall Back
4 PDFs: Guitar/Bass, Drum Ensemble, Piano, Xylophones

ABOUT THE AUTHOR

WILL SCHMID

Will Schmid holds a B.A. from Luther College and a Ph.D. from the Eastman School of Music. His public school teaching included general music, choral music and band, and he taught at Winona Sate University, the University of Kansas, and the University of Wisconsin-Milwaukee. Will is a past-president of the 100,000-member National Association for Music Education (MENC).

Schmid is a program author for Pearson's *Silver Burdett Making Music* series. He is the principal author of the world's #1 selling *Hal Leonard Guitar Method* and over one hundred other books/ folios/CDs/DVDs for drumming, guitar, banjo, strings, and choral. Dr. Schmid is also the principal author/editor of an 8-volume high school choral textbook, *Something New to Sing About* (Glencoe/G. Schirmer). He has given workshops throughout the United States and in Australia, Canada, Japan, Mexico and Europe. After a two-year $140,000 national pilot project in twenty schools nationwide, Dr. Schmid launched the *World Music Drumming* curriculum (included in Drumming Units of *Making Music* grades 6-8) which brings the excitement of African and Latin drumming and singing to schools throughout the United States. This curriculum is now in over 20,000 schools worldwide. Recent additions to the World Music Drumming publications (Hal Leonard) include *New Ensembles and Songs, More New Ensembles and Songs, Peanut Butter Jam* (for grades 2-5), *BeatBox*, and 24 original compositions and arrangements in the *World Music Drumming Choral Series*.

Dr. Schmid is the recipient of the 1996 Distinguished Alumnus Award from the Eastman School of Music. In 2002 he was named a Lowell Mason Fellow by NAfME and given the Distinguished Service Award from the Music Industry Conference (MIC). In 2006, he was named the inaugural winner of the DeLucia Prize for Innovation in Music Education given by the Mockingbird Foundation. In 2011, Will was given the Weston H. Noble award at Luther College.

During his presidency of MENC (1994-96), Dr. Schmid worked to reestablish the importance of active music making in schools and in America at large. MENC created new partnership initiatives in the areas of guitar, keyboards, strings, drumming, and singing as exemplified by the *Get America Singing . . . Again!* Campaign and the GAMA/NAMM/MENC-sponsored Teaching Guitar workshops.